Dandelions

by Mia Posada

Stars
in
the
Grass

🎵 CAROLRHODA BOOKS, INC./MINNEAPOLIS

This book is available in two editions:
Library binding by Carolrhoda Books, Inc., a division of Lerner Publishing Group
Soft cover by First Avenue Editions, an imprint of Lerner Publishing Group
241 First Avenue North
Minneapolis, MN 55401 U.S.A.

Website address: www.lernerbooks.com

Library of Congress Cataloging-in-Publication

Posada, Mia.
    Dandelions: stars in the grass / by Mia Posada.
                    p. cm.
    Summary: Rhyming text presents the dandelion, not as a weed, but as a flower of great beauty. Includes information about the flower, a recipe, and science activities.
    ISBN 1-57505-383-7 (lib. bdg. : alk. paper) ISBN 1-57505-399-3 (pbk. : alk. paper)
    1. Common dandelion—Juvenile literature. [1. Dandelions.] I. Title.
QK495.C74P67 2000
583'.99—dc21   98-53000

Manufactured in the United States of America
3 4 5 6 7 8 -JR- 07 06 05 04 03 02

To Raul

I know that some people
call it a **weed**,

but to me the dandelion
is a **noble**
breed.

Bright yellow petals
adorn each one,

spreading out
like rays of the sun.

In spring, dandelions bloom
like gold stars in the grass,

growing taller and taller
as the warm days pass.

Under sunny summer skies,

Index

Boldface page numbers refer to definitions of terms and page numbers followed by the italicized letter *f* indicate figures

A
Abstract, misunderstandings and, 117–118
Abstract language, **101**–104
Abstraction, ladder of, 102, 103*f*
Abuse. *See also* Aggression; Violence
  attachment styles from, 209–210
  in romantic relationships, 247–249
Acitelli, Linda, 26
Acknowledgment, **74**–75
Adams, John Quincy, 23
Adaptation, 176–197
  to audiences, 319–320
  as communication process, 178
  guidelines for, 191–197
  in organizations, 291–293
Advertising, 340–341
Advisory groups, 260
  objective of, 260
  at Petroleum Equipment Institute, 260
Affectional preference, 111
African Americans, 111
  artifacts and, 135
  code switching and, 197
  communication style of, 90, 188–189
  ideals about weight of women, 134
  interrupting and, 105
  listening style of, 161
  paralanguage and, 141

representation in media, 38
  storytelling and, 303
  use of Internet and, 363
Age, perception and, 59
The Age of Distraction (Urgo), 362
Aggression. *See also* Abuse; Violence
  vs. assertion and deference, 89, 89*f*
  passive. *See* Passive aggression
Alcohol, and failure to negotiate safe sex, 250
Ambiguity, in nonverbal communication, 126–127
Ambiguous language, **100**–101
Ambushing, **163**–164
American Sign Language (ASL), 153
Amusing Ourselves to Death (Postman), 339
Anderson, Rob, 375
Answering machines, 353
Anxious/ambivalent attachment, 210
Arab culture
  gift giving in, 136
  personal space in, 29
Arbitrary language, **98**–99
Aristotle, on public speaking, 22–23, 33
ARPAnet, 354
Artifacts, **135**–137
Asian Americans
  code switching and, 197
  representation in media, 38
  and use of Internet, 363
Asian culture. *See also* Japanese culture; Nepalese culture; Taiwanese culture; Vietnamese culture

avoiding overt disagreement in, 29, 100–101
  avoiding overt disinterest in, 128
  as collectivist culture, 64, 183
  communication style in, 90
  eye contact in, 131
  family relationships in, words describing, 184
  and feng shui, 139
  harmony in, 186
  and job interviews, 386
  respect of elderly in, proverb showing, 184
  silence in, 130
ASL. *See* American Sign Language
Assertion, *vs.* aggression and deference, 89, 89*f*
Assimilation, **195**
Attachment styles, 208–210, 209*f*
Attention, preserving focused, 361–362
Attraction, influences on, 238–239
Attributions, **56,** 56*f*, 68
Audioconferencing, 356–357
Authoritarian interviews, 382
Autonomy, **233**

B
Ball-Rokeach, Sandra, 343
Bargh, John, 60
Bates, Eric, 55
Bateson, Mary Catherine, 137
Baxter, Leslie, 43, 233
Becker, Anne, 340
Bell, Alexander Graham, 353
Berger, Peter, 195
Beyer, Janice, 286
Bingham, Shereen, 284
Birth mother, 98

Bisexuals, and social recognition, 183
The Blair Witch Project (film), 41
Blaming rites, 286
Blended families, 98
Body of speech, 313
Body posture. *See* Kinesics
Bolton, Robert, 157
Bormann, Ernest, 36
Bowen, Sheryl, 250
Bowlby, John, 208
Bracketing, **91**
Brainstorming, **259**
   rules for, 259*f*
Brainstorming groups
   facilitator in, 260
   objective of, 259
Brazil
   eye contact in, 131
   space in, 130
Brute facts, 104
Buber, Martin, 73
Buddhism, and social recognition, 183

C

Careers
   in communication, 44–46
   importance of communication in, 19–20
Carlos, John, 132
Cars, smart, 359
Cause-effect pattern of speeches, 314
Census Bureau. *See* U.S. Census Bureau
Centralized interaction patterns, in small groups, 267, 268*f*
Certainty, *vs.* provisionalism, 78–79
Chalk talk, 132
Children
   gender and games, 186–187
   influence of family on, 207–210
   lack of language and, 17
   mass communication and, 341
   television
      sexrole stereotypes and, 339
      violence in, 337
   wolfboy, 18
China, gift giving in, 136
Chinese word for crisis, 83
Chronemics, **138**–140. *See also* Time

Civic life, importance of communication in, 20–21
Civil rights movement, and development of communication field, 24, 25
Climate. *See* Communication climates
Climate communication, 269*f*, **270**
   example of, 271*f*
Closed questions, 382
Closedness, **234**
Closeness, self disclosure and, 214–215
Closing stage of interviews, 379–380
Clothing. *See* Artifacts
Co-cultures. *See* Social communities
Co-worker(s)
   friendship between, 295
   personal relationships among, 37
   romantic relationships between, 295
   self disclosure to, 215
Code switching, 197
Cognitive abilities, perception and, 60–63
Cognitive complexity, **61**
   perception and, 61–62
Cognitive restructuring, **319**
Cognitive schemata, **53**
   listening and, 155–156
Cohesion, **264**
   promoting, 265
   in small groups, 264–265
Collectivist culture, 64
   space and, 130
   view of personal identity in, 183
Collegial stories, 285–286
Commitment, **230**–231
   in friendship, 236
   in groups, 264
   vs. passion, 230
   in romantic relationships, 241
Communication, **28**
   careers in, 44–46
   climate. *See* Climate communication; Communication climates
   computer-mediated, 354–357
   cultural diversity and, 39–40, 90, 181–191
   with disabled people, 76
   downward, 290

egocentric, 269*f*, **270**–271
features of, 28–30
group and team. *See* Group and team communication
health and, 17–18
horizontal, 290
importance of, 4, 16–21
interpersonal. *See* Interpersonal communication
intrapersonal. *See* Intrapersonal communication
mass. *See* Mass communication
meanings and, 29–30
models of. *See* Models of communication
nonverbal. *See* Nonverbal communication
oral, **315**–316
organizational. *See* Organizational communication
person-centered, 192
personal identity and, 17, 203–207
and power, 25–26
principles of, 104–108
procedural, 269*f*, **270**
process of, **28**–29, 43–44
public. *See* Public communication
research in. *See* Research
skills, 6–7
symbolic, 29
systemic, 29, 178–181
task, **269**–270, 269*f*
technology. *See* Technology
telephone, 353–354
upward, 290
verbal. *See* Verbal communication
written, 315, 352–353
Communication apprehension, **317**–319
   causes of, 318
   reducing, 318–319
Communication climates, 44, 72–92, **73**
   continuum of, 74*f*
   defensive/supportive, 77–82
   improving, 88–92
   levels of confirmation/disconfirmation and, 73–77
   self disclosure. *See* Self disclosure
Communication continuum, 34, 35*f*

Communication field, 14–46
    breadth of, 33–42
    history of, 21–26
    unifying themes in, 42–44
Communication network, **290**–291
Communication rules. *See* Rules
Communication technology. *See*
    Technology
Comparative pattern of
    speeches, 314
Comparisons, as evidence,
    310, 311*f*
Complaint interviews, 377
Composing a Life (Bateson), 137
Computer conferencing, 358
Computer-mediated communica-
    tion, 354–357
Conclusion of speech, 313–314
Conference call, 357–358
Conferencing, 357–358
Confirmation, level of, communica-
    tion climate and, 73–77, 77*f*
Conflict, **82**–87
    components of, 84
    constructive, 274
    covert, **83**
    disruptive, 273–274
    effective timing of, 90–91
    labeling and, 57
    lose-lose approach to, 84
    management of, 83–87
    managing, in groups, 272–274
    outcomes of, 87
    overt, **83**
    reducing, problem orientation
        with, 80
    resolution of
        grace in, 91–92
        impact of family on, 105
    responses to, 86–87, 86*f*
    views of, 87
    win-lose approach to, 84–85
    win-win approach to, 85
Conflict resolution rites, 287
Conformity, as limitation to group,
    262–263
Congress, on privacy of Internet
    users, 366
Connection, **233**
Conquergood, Dwight, 27
Conrad, Charley, 28, 280, 289
Constitutive rules, **105**, 106, 231
    in groups/teams, 257–258
Constructive conflict, 274

Constructivism, **53**
Consulting, as career, 46
Content level of meaning, **30**
Control
    vs. problem orientation,
        80–81
    silence and, 130
Cookies, **366**
Corporate stories, 284
Counseling interviews, 376
Couples. *See* Marriage; Personal
    relationship(s); Romantic
    relationship(s)
Covert conflict, **83**
Cox, Bryan, 132
Cox, Robert, 137
Credibility, **307**
    derived, **307**
    initial, **307**
    terminal, **307**
Crisis, Chinese word for, 83
Critical listening, 164–167
    to mass communication, 344
    to speakers, 320–321
Critical research methods, **28**
Cultivation theory, **336**–339
    process of, 336–337
Cultural diversity
    communication and, 39–40, 90,
        181–191
    gift giving and, 136
    in interviews, 386
    listening and, 161
    in nonverbal communication,
        130–131
    process of responding to,
        195–197
Cultural relativism, **194**–195
Cultural stereotypes, represented
    in media, 38, 341
Cultural values, proverbs showing,
    184–185, 187
Culture, **64, 181**
    learning, through communica-
        tion, 182–183
    multiple, in single geographic
        location, 183–185
    perception and, 64
    reflected and sustained in com-
        munication, 189–190
Cyberhate, 357
Cybermemorials, 354
Cybersex, 354
Cyberspace. *See* Internet

D
Data Smog (Shenk), 360
Date rape, 98, 190, 248
Decentralized interaction patterns,
    in small groups, 267, 268*f*
Decision-making groups, 261
"The Declaration of Sentiments"
    (Stanton), 27
Defensive communication climates,
    77–82
Defensive listening, **163**
Deference, *vs.* aggression and
    assertion, 89, 89*f*
Definition, as symbolic ability,
    109–110
DeFleur, Melvin, 343
Demand-withdraw pattern,
    108, 108*f*
Democratic societies, communica-
    tion in, 21–22
Derived credibility, **307**
Description, *vs.* evaluation, 78
Descriptive statistics, as quantita-
    tive research method, 26
Dewey, John, 23, 262
Dialectics. *See* Relationship
    dialectics
Direct definition, 207
Disabilities, communicating with
    people with, 76
Disconfirmation, level of,
    communication climate and,
    73–77, 77*f*
Dismissive attachment, 209–210
Disruptive conflict, 273–274
Distance, dealing with, in
    personal relationships, 182,
    244–245, 246
Distributed power structure, in
    small groups, 266–267
Distributive interviews, 382
Domestic partners, 98
Downers, 223
Downward communication, 290
Dual-career relationships, 246–247
Duck, Steve, 18, 242
Dyadic breakdown, 238*f*, **242**
Dyadic phase of relationship break-
    down, 238*f*, **242**–243

E
E-mail. *See* Electronic mail
Eating
    music and, 138

Eating, *continued*
    as symbol, 42
Eating disorders
    media-created, in Fiji, 340
    society and, 218
EchoMail, 361
Edelstein, Alex, 334
Education
    as career, 44–45
    liberal, 22–24
EEOC. *See* Equal Employment
    Opportunity Commission
Effect-cause pattern of
    speeches, 314
Effenberg, Stefan, 132
Egan, Gerald, 168
Ego-surfing, 99
Egocentric communication, 269*f*,
    270–271
    example of, 271*f*
Electronic communities. *See*
    Virtual communities
Electronic epoch, **332**–333
Electronic mail, 355
    ethics of, 356
    tracking at work, 367
Emoticons, 99
Empathy, **63**
    vs. neutrality, 81
    vs. person-centeredness, 63
Employment interview(s),
    376–377. *See also* Hiring
    illegal questions in, 387–388
    research on company before, 385
Endorsement, **75**–77
Enhancement rites, 287
Enron scandal, 289
Entman, Ralph, 336
Entman, Robert, 38
Environmental distractions, **159**
Environmental factors, as nonver-
    bal communication, **138**
Environmental racism, 137
Epoch
    electronic, **332**–333
    literate, **330**–331
    print, **331**–332
    tribal, **330**
Equal Employment Opportunity
    Commission (EEOC), 387
Equality
    between partners and satisfac-
        tion with relationship, 246
    vs. superiority, 81–82

Equity, and satisfaction with
    relationship, 246
Ethics, **43**
    and communication, 41, 43
    of electronic mail, 356
    mindfulness and, 154
    organizations and, 289
Ethnicity. *See* Race and ethnicity
Ethnocentrism, **79, 194**
Ethnography, as qualitative
    research method, 27
Ethos, 22, 23*f*
Euphoria, 239
European Americans
    communication style of, 90, 188
    interrupting and, 105
    paralanguage and, 141
    use of Internet and, 363
Evaluation
    vs. description, 78
    static, **119**
Evidence, **309**–312
Examples, as evidence, 310, 311*f*
Exit interviews, 378
Exit response to conflict, 86, 86*f*
Expectations, perception and,
    59–60
Experiments, as quantitative
    research method, 26–27
Exploratory communication, in
    romantic relationships,
    238*f*, 239
Extemporaneous delivery of
    speeches, **316**
Eye contact
    cultural differences in, 125,
        131, 133
    of happy/unhappy couples, 128
    women and, 129
Eyewitness testimony, 68

F
Face motions. *See* Kinesics
Facilitator
    in brainstorming groups, 260
    in focus group, 259
Facsimile system, 353–354
Facts
    brute, 104
    distinguishing from inferences,
        66–67
    institutional, 104
Family. *See also* Personal
    relationship(s)

communication with members
    of, 207–210
conflict resolution and, 105
constitutive rules in, 231
cultural differences in, 64, 184
personal space and, 137
regulative rules in, 232
relationship dialectics in,
    233–235
segmentation and, 234
storytelling in, 303
Family and Medical Leave Act
    (1993), 293
Family quilt, 195–196
Fantasy themes, **36**
Fashionista, 99
Faulkner, Shannon, 329, 334
Fax, 353–354
Fearful attachment, 209
Federal Trade Commission
    (FTC), 366
Feedback, **31**
    in interactive model of commu-
        nication, 31, 32*f*
Feldman, Clyde, 84
Feng shui, 139
Field of experience
    in interactive model of commu-
        nication, 31, 32*f*
    in transactional models of com-
        munication, 32*f*, 33
Fiji, media-influenced dieting
    in, 340
First Amendment, 302
Flextime, 292
Focus groups
    facilitator in, 259
    objective of, 259
Food, as symbol, 42
Formal communication
    network, 290
Formal interviews, 380–381
Foucault, Michael, 25
Freedom of nonverbal
    speech, 132
Friendship(s). *See also* Personal
    relationship(s)
    between co-workers, 295
    commitment in, 236
    development of, 235–237
    honest feedback in, 88
    long-distance, 244–245
    nascent, 236
    regulative rules in, 232

relationship dialectics and, 233–235
segmentation and, 234
self disclosure in, 215
separation and, 234
stabilized, 236
between supervisors and subordinates, 37, 295
trust in, 236
types of, 236–237
waning, 236–237
FTC. *See* Federal Trade Commission
Funnel sequence, 379

G
Gandy, Oscar, 336
Gatekeeper, **335**
Gates, Henry Louis, 197
Gays
legal rights of, 183
managing domestic responsibilities, 247
society and, 216
Gender. *See also* Men; Women
children and games and, 186–187
dissatisfaction with relationship and, 242–243
listening styles and, 37–38, 155, 188
personal identity and, 216
primary basis of relationships and, 187–188
as social community, 186–187
space and, 129
stereotypes
parents communicating, 207
television and, 339
General semantics, 118
Generalization
in mass media, 102
qualifying, 118–119
Generalized other, 205–207
society as, 215–218
Generations at Play, 35
Geographic separation, coping with, 182, 245, 246
Gerbner, George, 337
Gibb, Jack, 77, 81
Gift giving, cultural differences in, 136
Gouran, Dennis, 36

Grace, **91**
in conflict resolution, 91–92
Grapevine, 291
Gratification, 333–334
Grave dressing in relationship breakdown, 238*f*, **244**
Griping, ritual of, 287–288
Gronbeck, Bruce, 29, 31
Group(s), **257**. *See also* Leadership
development of, 258–261
limitations of, 261–263
managing conflict in, 272–274
norms, 267–268
rules in, 257–258
share goals in, 257
size of, advantages/disadvantages, 265–266
small, features of, 264–268
strengths of, 263–264
vs. teams, 257
types of, 256
Group and team communication, 35–36, 254–274
challenges of, 269–274
fantasy themes in, 36
types of, 269–271, 269*f*
Groupthink, **265**

H
Hackers, 367
Hall, Edward T., 182
Halo effect, 310
Hamilton, Cheryl, 306
Haptics, **133**–134
cultural differences concerning, 130
power and, 134
women and, 129
Hasidic Jews, eye contact with women and, 133
Hayakawa, S. I., 102
Health, communication and, 17–18
Hearing, **153**
vs. listening, 153
Hegel, Georg Wilhelm Friedrich, 184
Hendrick, Clyde, 240
Hendrick, Susan, 240
Hierarchical language, 283
Hierarchical power structure, in small groups, 266–267
Hinduism, and social recognition, 183
Hiring. *See also* Employment interview(s)

discrimination in, 387
importance of communication and, 20
physical appearance and, 134
Hispanic Americans, 111
representation in media, 38, 341
and use of Internet, 363
Hispanic culture, as collectivist culture, 64
Historical research, as qualitative research method, 27
Homeless, and Public Electronic Network, 365
Homeostasis, **180**–181
Homes, smart, 359
Homophobia, 217–218
Homosexuality, 111. *See also* Gays; Lesbians
Horizontal communication, 290
Houston, Marsha, 193
Human relations, as career, 46
Hypothetical questions, 383
Hypothetical thought, **113**–114

I
I, 114–115
"I Have a Dream" (King), 27, 36
I language, 78, 120, 120*f*
and interpreting nonverbal communication, 144
in negotiating safe sex, 250
I-me dialogues, 115
ICA. *See* International Communication Association
Idealizing communication, in romantic relationships, 240
Identity. *See* Personal identity
Identity scripts, 207–208
Idioms, 166
Implantable memory chip, 97
Impromptu delivery of speeches, **316**
Income. *See* Socioeconomic status
Indexing, **119**
Indians, artifacts and, 135
Individualistic culture, 64. *See also* Western culture
space in, 130
Inference, **66**
distinguishing facts from, 66–67
Informal communication network, 290–291
Informal interviews, 380–381
Information, *vs.* knowledge, 360

Information-getting interviews, 375–376

Information-giving interviews, 375

Information overload, 359–361

Informational listening, 164–167

Ingham, Harry, 213

Initial credibility, **307**

Institutional facts, 104

Intensifying communication, in romantic relationships, 238*f*, 239–240

Interaction, in public speaking, 306

Interaction patterns, in small groups, 267
  centralized, 267, 268*f*
  decentralized, 267, 268*f*

Interactive models of communication, 31, 32*f*

Interconnectivity, **358**–359

Intercultural communication. *See* Cultural diversity, communication and

Internal obstacles to listening, 159–161

International Communication Association (ICA), 24

Internet, 354–357
  buying/selling stocks on, 357
  income and race, and use of, 363
  punctuation of communication on, 107
  regulating, 365–368

Interpersonal communication, 34–35
  emphasis on, 24

Interpretation, **56**–57, 104, **156**–157
  attributions, **56**, 56*f*
  of nonverbal communication, problems with, 143–145
  self-serving bias, **57**

Interrupting, 162

Interview(s)
  communication in, 374–388
  cultural diversity in, 386
  employment. *See* Employment interview(s)
  forms of questions in, 382–384
  illegal questions in, 387–388
  neutral communication in, 81
  nonverbal communication in, 387
  preparing for, 385–386
  purposes of, 375–378

as quantitative research method, 26
  silence in, 130
  structure of, 378–380
  styles of, 380–382

Intimacy
  navigating to sustain, 241
  relationship culture and, 241–242
  shared experiences and, 113–114
  whispering and, 140

Intrapersonal communication, **33**–34
  based on selective perception, examples of, 52
  challenges in, 218–224
  personal growth and, 219–224
  positive, 224
  self-sabotage as, 224

Intrapsychic phase in relationship breakdown, 238*f*, **243**

Introduction of speech, 312–313

Investment, commitment growing out of, 230

Invitational communication, in romantic relationships, 238, 238*f*

Irritainment, 99

Isocrates, 22

J

Jackson, Jesse, 195

Japanese culture
  eye contact in, 125
  negotiation styles in, 100–101, 117

Jews
  Hasidic, eye contact with women and, 133
  ritual of griping among, 287–288
  and traditions of, 183

Job interview(s). *See* Employment interview(s)

Johari Window, 213–214, 214*f*

Jones, Steven, 364

Joy, Bill, 359

Judgment, avoiding in relationship listening, 168

K

Katriel, Tamar, 287

Kennedy, Randall, 111

Kenya, gift giving in, 136

Killenberg, George, 375

Kinesics, **131**–133
  liking and responsiveness, 133
  openness and, 133
  reflecting moods, 132

King, Martin Luther, Jr., "I Have a Dream" speech, 27, 36

Kiturim, 287–288

Knowledge, *vs.* information, 360

Korzybski, Alfred, 102, 118

Kruger, Pamela, 154

Kurt Lewin, 8

L

Labels, 109–110
  negative
    in marital conflicts, 57
    in romantic relationships, 110
    and self-esteem, 207
  positive, and self-esteem, 207
  totalizing, **109**

Language, 98–108
  abstract, **101**–104
  of abusers, 248–249
  ambiguous, **100**–101
  arbitrary, **98**–99
  certainty, 78–79
  changes in, 98–99
  creating meaning, 104
  creating reality, 98
  defining phenomena, 109–110
  defining relationships and interaction, 116
  descriptive, 78
  evaluating phenomena, 110–112
  features of, 98–104
  general, 102–103
  hierarchical, 283
  I. See I language
  importance of, 96–97
  loaded, **111**
  masculine, 283–284
  normalizing sexual harassment, 284
  organizing perceptions, 112
  private, of couples, 240
  provisional, 79
  qualifying, 118–119
  of race and ethnicity, 103
  reappropriating, 111
  self-reflection, 114–115
  tentative, 67
  thinking hypothetically, 113–114

Whorf-Sapir view of, 110
You, 120, 120*f*
Laswell, Harold, 30
Latinas/Latinos, 111. *See also*
     Hispanic Americans;
     Hispanic culture
Leadership, 271–272
Leading questions, 384
Learning, and Western culture, 206
Leo, John, 341
Lesbians
     legal rights of, 183
     managing domestic
          responsibilities, 247
     society and, 216
Letters, advantages/disadvantages
     of, 352–353
Levinson, Paul, 333
Lewin, Kurt, 335
Liberal education, 22–24
Lightner, Candace, 305
Liking
     in nonverbal communication,
          129, 133
     in verbal communication, 116
Linear models of communication,
     30, 30*f*
Listening, **44,** 150–171
     ambushing, **163**–164
     amount of time spent daily, 152
     critical, 164–167, 320–321
     cultural diversity and, 161
     defensive, **163**
     to discriminate, 171
     effective, guidelines for, 164–171
     ethical responsibility of, 156
     gender and, 37–38, 155, 188
     vs. hearing, 153
     importance of, 152
     ineffective, 152
          forms of, 161–164
     informational, 164–167
     literal, **164**
     monopolizing and, **162**
     Mother Teresa on, 152
     obstacles to, 158–164
     for pleasure, 171
     process of, 153–158, 153*f*
     pseudolistening, **161**–162
     relationship, 167–171
     responsive, 157
     selective, **163**
Literal listening, **164**
Literate epoch, **330**–331

Loaded language, **111**
Loaded questions, 384
Logos, 22, 23*f*
Long-distance relationships,
     244–245, 246
     communication technology
          sustaining, 182
     lack of small talk and, 19, 245
Looking glass self. *See* Reflected
     appraisal
Lose-lose approach to conflict, 84
Loyalty response to conflict, 86,
     86*f,* 87
Luft, Joseph, 213

M

MADD. *See* Mothers Against
     Drunk Driving
Mainstreaming, **336**–337
Management, as career, 46
Manuscript delivery of
     speeches, **316**
Marriage. *See also* Personal
     relationship(s); Romantic
     relationship(s)
     conflicts in, labeling and, 57
     dissatisfaction and intonation,
          140–141
     dual-career, 246–247
     importance of communication
          in, 18–19
     institution of, in Western
          culture, 206
     interrupting in, 106–107
     relationship talk in, experiment
          on, 26–27
     same-sex, 219
          and society, 216
     sharing housework in, 101
     similarity of personality and
          happiness, 239
     tension in, mind reading and, 65
Masculine language, 283–284
Mass communication, 38,
     328–345, **329**
     career in, 45
     challenges for interacting with,
          342–345
     and children, 341
     constructing news, 335
     cultural stereotypes represented
          in, 38, 341
     defining people and events, 110
     evolution of, 330–333, 330*f*

functions and effects of,
     333–341
     as generalized other, 206
     overgeneralization in, 102
McChesney, Robert, 340
McLuhan, Marshall, 330–333
Me, 114–115
Mead, George Herbert, 17, 114, 203
Mean world syndrome, **339**
Meaning, **30**–31, 42–43, 98–108
     content level of, **30**
     interpretation and, 104
     punctuation and, 107–108
     relationship level of, **30**
Media. *See* Mass communication
Media literacy, developing,
     342–344, 342*f*
Meeks, Brenda, 240
"Melting pot," 195
Memorized delivery of speeches, **316**
Memory. *See* Remembering
Memos, advantages/disadvantages
     of, 352–353
Men. *See also* Gender
     artifacts and, 135
     communication style of, 155, 187
     control and, 116
     dissatisfaction in romantic rela-
          tionship, 242–243
     listening styles of, 37–38,
          155, 188
     and paralanguage, 141
     primary basis of relationships,
          187–188
     relationship talk and,
          26–27, 187
     representation in media, 38
     showing liking with nonverbal
          communication, 129
     society and physical appearance
          of, 218
     and space, 129, 137
     touching and, 134
     violence/abuse against women,
          247–249
Message complexity, **158**–159
Message overload, **158**
Mexican Americans, code
     switching, 197
Michal-Johnson, Paula, 250
Mind reading, **65**
Mindfulness, **153**–154
     enhancing communication
          with, 154

Mindfulness, *continued*
  ethics and, 154
  in informational/critical
    listening, 165
  in relationship listening, 168
Minimal encouragers, **168**–169
Mirror interviews, 381
Mirror questions, 383
Mnemonic devices to improve
    memory, 166
Models of communication, 30–33
  interactive, 31, 32*f*
  linear, 30, 30*f*
  transactional, 31–33, 32*f*
Mojave tribe, sexual identity
    in, 217
Molloy, Jennifer, 302, 319
Monitoring, **67**–68
  and *I* and *me,* 115
  nonverbal communication, 143
  self-serving bias, 67–68
Monopolizing, **162**
Mother Teresa, on listening, 152
Mothers Against Drunk Driving
    (MADD), 305
Motivated sequence pattern of
    speeches, 314
Motley, John, 302
Motley, Michael, 319
Multilingualism, **197**
Multitasking, **361**–362

N
Nascent friendship, 236
National Association of Colleges
    and Employers, 20
National Association of Teachers of
    Public Speaking, 23
National Communication
    Association, 24
National Council on Alcoholism
    and Drug Dependence, 250
Native American culture
  artifacts and, 135
  silence and, 130
Navajo, code talkers, 182
Navajo tribe, sexual identity in, 217
Navigating, to sustain intimacy, 241
Negative attributions, 68
Neglect response to conflict, 86, 86*f*
Nepalese culture, listening in, 161
Networking, 280–281
Neutrality, *vs.* empathy, 81
Neutralization, **234**

News, construction of, 335
9/11 terrorist attack, 97, 350–351
Noise, **30**
  in linear model of communica-
    tion, 30, 30*f*
  in transactional models of com-
    munication, 32, 32*f*
Nonverbal communication, 44, **98,**
    124–145
  ambiguity and, 126–127
  conveying strategy with, 80
  dissatisfaction and, 133
  effective, guidelines for, 143–145
  establishing relationship-level
    meanings with, 128–130
  freedom of, 132
  interacting with public
    speeches, 306
  interacting with verbal commu-
    nication, 127
  interpreting, problems with,
    143–145
  in interviews, 387
  lack of, in computer
    conferencing, 358
  of listening, 157
  minimal encouragers, 169
  monitoring, 143
  principles of, 126–131
  reflecting cultural values,
    130–131
  regulating interaction with,
    127–128
  responsiveness in, 128
  share of, in communication, 126
  turning descriptive words into
    evaluative message with, 78
  types of, 131–142
Nonverbal rites, 286
Norm(s), **267**–268
Novelty, **233**–234

O
O'Donnell-Trujillo, Nick, 284, 287
Offices, smart, 359
Open questions, 382
Opening stage of interviews,
    378–379
Openness, **234**
  of systems, **180**
Oral style of communication,
    315–316
  vs. written style, 315
Orbe, Mark, 188

Organization of perceptions,
    53–56, 112
  personal constructs, **54**
  prototypes, **53**
  scripts, **55**–56
  stereotypes, **54**–55
Organizational charts, 289
Organizational communication,
    37–38, 278–296
  challenges of, 291–296
  and ethics, 289
  features of, 280–282
Organizational culture, **37,**
    282–291
  rites and, 286–287
  rituals and, 287–288
  sexual harassment and, 28, 37
  stories and, 284–286
  structures and, 288–291
  vocabulary and, 283–284
Organizational pattern of
    speeches, 314
Overt conflict, **83**
The Oxford Dictionary, 99

P
Pacanowsky, Michael, 284, 287
Paralanguage, **140**–141
Paraphrasing, **169**
Parents. *See* Family
Participation, **196**
  cohesion and, 265
  and cultural diversity, 196–197
Particular others, 205
  family, 207–210
  peers, 210–215
Passion, **230**
  vs. commitment, 230
Passive aggression
  vs. assertion, 89
  as covert conflict, 83
Pathos, 22, 23*f*
Peers, communication with,
    210–215
PEN. *See* Public Electronic
    Network
Perception, **43,** 50–68, **51**
  checking, 65–66
  of eyewitness, 68
  improving, 65–68
  influences on, 58–64
  processes of, 51–58
Performance reviews, 377
  conducting research before, 385

Performance studies, 35
Person-centeredness, **62,** 192
  vs. empathy, 63
  perception and, 62–63
  preparing for interview and, 385–386
Personal constructs, **54**
  listening and, 156
Personal growth
  and intrapersonal communication, 219–224
  self disclosure and, 214
Personal growth groups, 256
Personal identity, 202–224
  development of, in communication, 17, 203–207
  family and, 207–210
  peers and, 210–215
  society and, 215–218
Personal relationship(s), 228–250, **229.** *See also* Family; Friendship(s); Marriage; Romantic relationship(s)
  among co-workers, 37, 294–296
  conflict in, 83
  dealing with distance in, 244–245, 246
  demand-withdraw pattern in, 108, 108*f*
  dialectical tensions in, 234
  evolution of, 235–244
  features of, 229–235
  hypothetical thought and, 113–114
  importance of communication in, 18–19
  rules in, 231–232
  vs. social relationship, 230
  society's views on, 232
  as systems, 180
  time spent together and, 140
  use of general language in, 103
Personal rituals, 287
Personal space. *See* Space
Personal stories, 285
Personalized communication, in romantic relationships, 240
Persuasion, 22, 23*f*
Persuasive interviews, 376
Petroleum Equipment Institute, advisory groups at, 260
Pezzullo, Phaedra, 25
Physical appearance, **134**–135

and media, in Fiji, 340
  society and, 134, 218
Physiological factors, perception and, 58–59
Physiological state, perception and, 58–59
Plato, 22, 27
Policies, **290**
Polito, Lou, 287
Poole, Marshall Scott, 280, 289
Porter, Richard, 40
Positive attributions, 68
Positive visualization, **60,** 61, **319**
Postman, Neil, 339
Potter, W. James, 340
Power, **266**
  balance of, in interviews, 381–382
  communication and, 25–26
  haptics and, 134
  in nonverbal communication, 129–130
  space and, 134, 137
  in verbal communication, 116
Power over, **266**
Power structure, in small groups, 266–267
  distributed, 266–267
  hierarchical, 266–267
Power to, **266**
Predictability, **233**–234
Prejudgments, 160
Preoccupation, 160
Price, Reynolds, 111
Print epoch, **331**–332
Privacy
  of Internet users, 365–368
  need for, 234
Probing questions, 384
Problem orientation, *vs.* control, 80–81
Problem-solution pattern of speeches, 314
Problem solving, standard agenda for, 262*f*
Problem-solving interviews, 376
Procedural communication, 269*f*, **270**
  example of, 271*f*
Professional life, importance of communication in, 19–20
Project teams, 258–259
"Proofs," 22
Prototypes, **53**

Provisionalism, *vs.* certainty, 78–79
Proxemics, **137**–138
  gender and, 129
  power and, 134
Proximity, and attraction, 238
Pseudolistening, **161**–162
Psychological responsibility, of women, **247**
Public communication, 36, 300–321
  adapting to audiences, 319–320
  challenges in, 317–321
  credibility and, 307
  critics of, 36
  as enlarged conversation, 302–306
  features of, 305–306
  specific purpose in, 308
  thesis statement in, 308
Public Electronic Network (PEN), 364
  and homeless, 365
Public speech(es)
  cause-effect pattern of, 314
  comparative pattern of, 314
  delivery of, 315–316
    styles of, 316
  effect-cause pattern of, 314
  entertaining, 303
  evidence in, **309**–312
  informative, 304–305
  motivated sequence pattern of, 314
  narrative, 303
  organizational pattern of, 314
  organizing, 312–315
  persuasive, 305
  planning for, 308
  problem-solution pattern of, 314
  purposes of, 302–305
  spatial pattern of, 314
  temporal pattern of, 314
  topical pattern of, 314
Puerto Rico, touching in, 130
Puffery, 341
Punctuation, **107**–108

Q
Qualitative research methods, **27**
Quality circles, **260**–261
Quantitative research methods, **26**–27
Question(s)
  closed, 382
  hypothetical, 383

Question(s), *continued*
  illegal, 387–388
  in interviews, 382–384
  leading, 384
  mirror, 383
  open, 382
  probing, 384
  summary, 384
Questionnaires, as quantitative
  research method, 26
Quotations, as evidence, 310, 311*f*

R
Race and ethnicity
  languages of, 103
  method of classifying, dilemma
    on, 55
  personal identity and, 215
  as social community, 188–189
  and use of Internet, 363
Racism
  environmental, 137
  in media, 336
Rakow, Lana, 28
Rawlins, Bill, 235
Reality
  language creating, 98
  virtual, 351
Reappropriating language, 111
Recognition, **74**
Recognition rite, 287
Reflected appraisal, peers, 210–211
Reflective thinking, model
  of, 262*f*
Reframing, **234**
Regulative rules, **105,** 106, 232
  in groups/teams, 258
Relationship(s). *See* Friendship(s);
  Marriage; Personal relation-
  ship(s); Romantic relation-
  ship(s)
Relationship culture, **241**–242
Relationship dialectics, **233**–235
  in romantic relationships,
    241–242
  types of, 233–234
Relationship-enhancing attribu-
  tions, 68
Relationship level of meaning, **30**
Relationship listening, 167–171
Remembering, **157**–158
  enhancing, 166
Renewal rites, 287
Reprimand interviews, 377

Research
  in communication, 26–28
    advent of, 24
    as career, 44
    critical, **28**
    qualitative, **27**
    quantitative, **26**–27
  conducting for interviews, 385
  before public speaking, 306
Resistance, and cultural diversity,
  195–196
Resonance, **336**–337
Respect, 192–193, **196**
Responding, 150–171, **157**
  to mass communication,
    344–345
Responsiveness
  in nonverbal communication,
    128, 133
  in verbal communication, 116
Reverse attribution patterns, 68
Revising communication, in romantic relationships, 238*f*, 241
Rhetoric, 21–22. *See also* Public
  communication; Public
  speech(es)
  Aristotle on, 22–23, 33
  in liberal education, 23
Rich Media, Poor Democracy
  (McChesney), 340
Ridley, Carl, 84
Riot Grrrls, 111
Rites
  and organizational culture,
    286–287
  vs. rituals, 287
  types of, 286–287
Rituals
  and organizational culture,
    287–288
  vs. rites, 287
  types of, 287–288
Roles, **288**–289
  organizational, 288–289
Romantic relationship(s). *See
  also* Marriage; Personal
  relationship(s)
  abuse/violence in, 247–249
  body language and dissatisfac-
    tion in, 133
  between co-workers, 295
  constitutive rules in, 231
  desire for autonomy/
    connection, 233

development of, 237–244, 238*f*
  (un)happiness in
    attribution styles and, 68
    eye contact and, 128
    interdependent/independent
      and personal space, 137
  long-distance, 244–245, 246
  negative labeling in, 110
  negotiating safer sex in, 249–250
  novelty/predictability in, 234
  openness/closedness in, 234
  reframing and, 234
  regulative rules in, 232
  segmentation and, 234
  self disclosure in, 215
  separation and, 234
Rothenberg, David, 360
Routines, in romantic
  relationships, 242
Rubin, Lillian, 237
Rules, **231**–232
  constitutive, **105,** 106, 231
  in groups/teams, 257–258
  organizational, 289–290
  in personal relationships,
    231–232
  regulative, **105,** 106, 232
  in romantic relationships, 242

S
Same-sex marriage, 219
  and society, 216
Samovar, Larry, 40
Schemata. *See* Cognitive schemata
Schutz, Astrid, 57
Scripts, **55**–56
  identity, 207–208
  for responding, 156
Searle, John, 104
Secure attachment, 208–209
Segmentation, **234**
Selection, 52–53
Selective listening, **163**
Self, 203
  development of, in communica-
    tion, 203–207
  family and, 207–210
  peers and, 210–215
  society and, 215–218
Self-concept
  distorted, 221
  downers and, 223
  healthy, 214, 221
  improving, 221

peers and, 211
uppers and, 223
vultures and, 223–224
Self disclosure, 212–215
    and closeness, 214–215
    Johari Window, 213–214, 214f
    and personal growth, 214
    and relationship
        development, 215
    and self-concept, 214
Self-esteem, and positive/negative
    labels, 207
Self-fulfilling prophesy, 203–204
    positive, disadvantaged stu-
        dents and, 204
Self-sabotage, 224
Self-serving bias, **57**
    monitoring, 67–68
Self-talk. *See* Intrapersonal
    communication
Selling Out America's Children
    (Walsh), 341
Sensory abilities, differences in,
    perception and, 58
Separation, **234**
Sex, safer
    negotiating, 249–250
    reasons for not practicing,
        249–250
Sexrole stereotypes
    parents communicating, 207
    and television, 339
Sexual harassment, 190
    language normalizing, 284
    and organizational culture,
        28, 37
Sexual identity, Navajo and Mojave
    tribes, 217
Sexual orientation, 111. *See also*
    Gays; Lesbians
    personal identity and, 216
Sexual preference, 111
Shannon, Claude, 30
Sharpe, Rochelle, 385
Shenk, David, 360
Signorielli, Nancy, 338
Silence, **141**–142
    exerting control with, 130
    at interviews, 130
    meanings of, 141–142
Similarity
    and attraction, 239
    cohesion and, 265
Sirkin, Louis, 132

Situational obstacles to listening,
    158–159
Skills training, **319**
Small group communication.
    See Group and team
        communication
Small talk
    lack of, in long-distance rela-
        tionships, 19, 245
    opening interviews with,
        378–379
Smart cars, 359
Smart homes, 359
Smart offices, 359
Smith, Tommie, 132
Social climbing, **267**
Social communities, **185**–189
    communication in, 256
    gender as, 186–187
    racial/ethnic groups as, 188–189
    social classes as, 188
    vs. subcultures, 185
Social comparison, 211–212
Social groups. *See* Social
    communities
Social perspectives, reflecting criti-
    cally on, 218–219
Social phase of relationship break-
    down, 238f, **243**
Social relationship, **230**
    vs. personal relationship, 230
Social rituals, 287–288
Social roles, perception and, 63–64
Social support phase in relation-
    ship breakdown, 238f
Society
    eating disorders and, 218
    gays and, 216
    as generalized other, 215–218
    lesbians and, 216
    physical appearance of men
        and, 218
    same-sex marriage and, 216
    views on personal relationships
        and, 232
Socioeconomic status
    personal identity and, 216–217
    as social community, 188
    and use of Internet, 363
Socrates, 27
Sophists, 22
South America, time in, 140
Space, 136–137
    gender and, 129

    in individualistic culture, 130
    power and, 134
Spatial pattern of speeches, 314
Speaking anxiety, **317**–319
Specific purpose, **308**
Speech(es). *See* Public communica-
    tion; Public speech(es)
Speech Association of America, 24
Speech Communication Associa-
    tion, 24
Speed
    emphasis on, 64
    in Western culture, 139–140
Spontaneity, *vs.* strategy, 79–80
Spouses. *See* Marriage; Personal
    relationship(s); Romantic
    relationship(s)
St. Augustine, 27
Stabilized friendship, 236
Standpoint, **183**
Standpoint theory, **183**
Stanton, Elizabeth Cady, 27
Star structure of speeches, 313
Static evaluation, **119**
Statistics, as evidence, 310, 311f
Status, time and, 138–139
Stereotypes, **54**–55, 112
    cultural, represented in media,
        38, 341
    listening and, 156
    sexrole
        parents communicating, 207
        and television, 339
    vs. totalizing, 109
Stories
    collegial, 285–286
    corporate, 284
    and organizational culture,
        284–286
    personal, 285
    war, **284**
Strategy, *vs.* spontaneity, 79–80
Stress interviews, 378, 382
Strine, Mary, 28, 284
Structures, **288**
    and organizational communica-
        tion, 280
    and organizational culture,
        288–291
    types of, 288–291
Subcultures, *vs.* co-cultures, 185
Substantive stage of interviews, 379
Suler, John, 356
Summary questions, 384

Superiority, *vs.* equality, 81–82
Supportive communication climates, 77–82
Surveys, as quantitative research method, 26
Switzerland, gift giving in, 136
Symbolic abilities, 108–116, 109*f*
Symbolic activities, 42
Symbols, **29,** 42
Synergy, **263**
Systematic desensitization, **318**
Systems, **29,** 178–181
    homeostasis, **180**–181
    interrelated, 178–179
    more than sum of its parts, 180
    openness, **180**
    organized wholes, 179

T
Taiwanese culture, contradicting in, 40
Task communication, **269**–270, 269*f*
    example of, 271*f*
Task groups
    communication in, 256
    types of, 258–261
Task rituals, 288
Taylor, Brian, 28
Team(s), **257**
    challenges of communication in, 269–274
    development of, 258–261
    vs. groups, 257
    rules in, 257–258
Teamwork, importance of, 258
Technology, 38–39, 350–368
    challenges of, 359–368
    interconnectivity and, **358**–359
    social critics of, 363–364
    sustaining long-distance relationships, 182
    understanding, 352–359
Telecommuting, 182, 292, 354
Teleconferencing, **357**–358
Telephone communication, 353–354
Television, gender stereotypes and, 339
Television advertisements, critical analysis of, 28
Temporal pattern of speeches, 314
Tentative language, 67
Terminal credibility, **307**
Territoriality. *See* Space

Terrorist attack of 9/11, 97, 350–351
Testimony, eyewitness, 68
Textual analysis, as qualitative research method, 27
Thesis statement, **308**
Time, 138–140
    amount of, spent daily on listening, 152
    as limitation to group, 262
    and personal relationships, 140
    in South America, 140
    and status, 138–139
    in transactional models of communication, 32, 32*f*
    in Western culture, 130, 139–140
Time pattern of speeches. *See* Temporal pattern of speeches
Tolerance, **196**
    and cultural diversity, 196
Topical pattern of speeches, 314
Totalizing, **109**
    vs. stereotyping, 109
Touching, 134
    cultural differences concerning, 130
    power and, 134
    women and, 129
Traditional communities, *vs.* virtual communities, 364–365
Training, as career, 46
Transactional models of communication, 31–33, 32*f*
Transition, **315**
Tribal epoch, **330**
Trice, Harrison, 286
Trust, in friendship, 236

U
Understanding, **196**
    and cultural diversity, 196
United States
    demographics of, in twenty-first century, 12
    eye contact in, 125, 131
    as "family quilt," 195–196
    individualistic culture of, 64
    as "melting pot," 195
    negotiation styles in, 117
    personal space in, 130, 137
    touching in, 130
    winning, proverbs showing, 185
Uppers, 223
Upward communication, 290
Urgo, Joseph, 361, 362

U.S. Census Bureau, dilemma on classifying races, 55
Uses and gratification theory, **333**–334

V
Verbal communication, 44, 96–120, **98.** *See also* Language
    guidelines for effective, 117–120
    importance of, 96–97
    nonverbal communication interacting with, 127
Videoconferencing, 358
Vietnamese culture, storytelling in, 303
Violence. *See also* Abuse; Aggression
    and communication, 248–249
    cycle of, 248, 248*f*
    in media, 337–339
    in romantic relationships, 247–249
Virtual communities
    ethical questions concerning, 365
    lack of face-to-face contact in, 365
    and narcissism, 364
    vs. traditional communities, 364–365
Virtual reality, 351
Visual aids, as evidence, 310, 311*f*
Vocabulary, organizational culture and, 283–284
Vocal cues, 140–141
Voice mail, 353
Voice response to conflict, 86–87, 86*f*
Von Bertalanffy, Ludwig, 179
Vultures, 223–224

W
Wall Street Journal, on advisory groups at Petroleum Equipment Institute, 260
Waning friendship, 236–237
War stories, **284**
Wave pattern of speeches, 313
Weaver, Warren, 30
Weight
    cultural ideals about, 134, 218
    and media, in Fiji, 340
West, Candice, 126
Western culture. *See also* Individualistic culture
    conflict/competition in, 186

expressing disinterest with
nonverbal communication
in, 128
family relationships in, words
describing, 184
gender roles in, 216
ideals about physical appearance in, 134–135, 218
institution of marriage in, 206
job interviews, 386
learning in, 206
showing liking with nonverbal
communication in, 129
time in, 130, 139–140
youth, words associated
with, 184
Whispering, 140
Whorf-Sapir view of language, 110
Win-lose approach to conflict,
84–85
Win-win approach to conflict, 85
Winans, James, 302

Wittgenstein, Ludwig, 96
Women. *See also* Gender
artifacts and, 135
code switching, 197
communication style of,
155, 187
control and, 116
cultural ideals about weight of,
134, 218
dissatisfaction in romantic relationships, 242–243
eating disorders and,
218, 340
eye contact and, 129
listening styles of, 37–38,
155, 188
and paralanguage, 141
primary basis of
relationships, 188
psychological responsibility
of, **247**
relationship talk and, 26–27, 187

representation in media, 38
showing liking with nonverbal
communication, 129
and space, 129, 137
touching and, 134
violence/abuse against, 247–249
Women's movement, and development of communication field,
24, 25
Written communication, 352–353
advantages/disadvantages of,
352–353
vs. oral, 315
Wydra, Nancilee, 139

Y
You language, 120, 120*f*

Z
Zeno of Citium, 172
Zimmerman, Don, 126
Zorn, Ted, 37, 294